Herbert W. Chilstrom

Hebrews
A NEW & BETTER WAY

FORTRESS PRESS   PHILADELPHIA

To Corinne
wife and best friend

Library of Congress Cataloging in Publication Data

Chilstrom, Herbert W., 1931–
   Hebrews—a new and better way.

   1. Bible. N.T. Hebrews—Criticism, interpretation,
etc. I. Title.
BS2775.2.C48   1984   227´.8706   83–5600
ISBN 0-8006-1717-7

K364E83   Printed in the United States of America   1–1717

Contents

A Word to the Reader

The New Testament author who wrote the Letter to the Hebrews has been my good friend for over two decades. Our friendship came about quite by accident. In the fall of 1962 I found myself serving on the faculty of a small college in the East. The professor who had regularly taught the course in Hebrews died shortly before my arrival. Because the course had already been announced in the catalog, somebody had to teach it. When the dean noted that my class load was a bit smaller than that of other teachers, he asked me to take over the course.

For the next several weeks I plunged feverishly into a study of this somewhat unfamiliar epistle, trying to ready myself for the opening of the term. I suspect that the students who showed up for my course that first year may not have gotten their money's worth. But in subsequent years, through my continuing work in the classroom, through my preaching and teaching in congregations and formal study at Princeton Theological Seminary, this remarkable epistle became a familiar treasure.

I invite you now to journey with me through the Letter to the Hebrews. I want you to meet my friend—the author of the letter. I want him to become your friend too.

Discovering a Treasure

Each time I teach the Book of Hebrews I begin by asking for a show of hands: How many of you have studied Hebrews in a formal classroom setting? One or two. How many of you have led a series of Bible studies on Hebrews in the congregation? Three or four. How many of you—I usually ask the pastors—have ever preached on a text from Hebrews? Five or six. In any group of twenty-five or thirty people, these are typical responses. Christians are largely unfamiliar with Hebrews.

If Hebrews is one of the lesser-known books in the New Testament, the reason is not hard to find. Anyone reading through the New Testament has probably, on reaching this book, experienced the feeling of having run into a brick wall. After traveling quickly and easily through the Gospels, the Acts of the Apostles, and the epistles of Paul, readers encounter in the very first chapter of Hebrews a language and pattern of thought so abstract and confusing that we are almost tempted to skip the rest of the book and go on to the seemingly safe and more comfortable Book of James.

The secret for handling Hebrews, of course, is to know a little about the epistle before we begin to read it. As with any storehouse of precious gems, we discover the treasure inside if we know the combination of the lock that must be opened for gaining admittance.

Here, then, are some clues I have discovered to unlock this Letter to the Hebrews and facilitate access to its treasure:

(1) Find two or three hours when you can read the epistle

through in one sitting. With pencil in hand, underscore the words *new, superior, better,* and *more excellent* each time you encounter them. These words provide your first clue. Most scholars believe that the epistle was originally addressed to Christians of Jewish background. Steeped in the Scriptures from earliest childhood, these Christians had a deep appreciation for their Hebrew roots. Without deprecating that rich heritage, the author of Hebrews wants them to know that in Christ we now have a new, superior, better, and more excellent way.

(2) The second clue follows from the first. There is an old saying about how the two Testaments of our Christian Bible relate to one another:

The new is in the old concealed;
The old is in the new revealed.

That understanding of the connection seems to fit the thought pattern of Hebrews. The author of the epistle sees no wall of separation between the old covenant and the new. The old covenant is by no means worthless; it is simply inadequate. In fact, the writer of the letter believes that the old covenant points beyond itself, anticipating and yearning for the new. This new covenant is fulfilled in Jesus Christ.

(3) The third clue again follows quite naturally. If Christ is the fulfillment of a new and better covenant, it is natural to ask how or in what way he has fulfilled it. In Hebrews, the answer is twofold: Jesus is the perfect high priest and Jesus is the perfect sacrifice. Out of their Old Testament background the Christians to whom this message was first addressed knew that the covenant with God required both priest for intercession and sacrifice for atonement. In Christ, they learn, both needs are met. Only in this Letter to the Hebrews are these two strands of fulfillment—priest and sacrifice—drawn together. The lines of a familiar Communion hymn are drawn directly from this message:

Offered was he for greatest and for least,
Himself the victim; himself the priest.

(4) Another significant clue has to do with the date of the

writing. It is important to understand that this Letter to the Hebrews was probably not written until late in the first century—around A.D. 80 or 90. This late origin makes it one of the last books of the New Testament to be written. It was addressed to believers who may have been in the Christian community for as long as forty to fifty years. In fact, some of the original readers may have been second-generation believers, people who grew up as Christians, perhaps taking the faith for granted. This clue is extremely important because it helps us to understand the letter's repeated warnings against spiritual laxity.

(5) It is also important to recognize that the pattern of the letter is quite different from that of other books in the New Testament. Hebrews begins like an oration and continues like an epistle, a letter which is then interrupted four times by a "sermonette"—at points where the author is so moved by a particular idea that the writing just "soars off" into a passionate discourse before returning to the main line of thought. The outline of the letter, with its pattern of discourses, is suggested already in the Table of Contents.

(6) Finally, a word about my friend, my unknown friend, the writer of Hebrews. Unlike the other New Testament epistles, Hebrews makes no mention of the author's name at the very outset. For this reason speculation has run rampant concerning the identity of the writer. Guesses have ranged all the way from Paul or Barnabas to Luke, Apollos, or even Silas. Some interpreters have suggested that Hebrews may have been written by a woman, who hid her identity in order that her book might find acceptance in the male-dominated church of the first century. Some portions of the book seem clearly to have been written by an author different from the writer of other portions. So the questions are many; for example, one author or more than one? male or female? Nobody knows for sure. To keep from tripping over my pronouns in the pages ahead I will simply refer to the writer(s) of the book (or passage) as "he."

What can we say about this unknown person? He is well educated, fully conversant with the Hebrew Scriptures, known to his readers, and probably a Jew. New Testament scholars say

9

that his writing style—in the original Greek—is the best to be found in the whole New Testament, surpassing even that of Luke. Here then is a skilled writer who knows what needs to be said and says it with brevity and beauty.

With these few clues to the treasure, come join me now for a step-by-step walk with my unknown friend, who has given us this remarkable portion of our Christian Scriptures, the Letter to the Hebrews.

1:1—2:4

The Son of God—Our Lord

1:1-4

These opening four verses stand as a theme or summary for the entire epistle. "In many and various ways God spoke of old": The author here affirms the validity of the old covenant. It was God who fashioned the covenant. God was actively involved with the people of Israel. They were his covenant people.

"But in these last days he has spoken to us by a Son": The author here points to the new and better covenant that has been established. It flows out of the old and supercedes it in the sense that God's plan for the world is now to be fulfilled in Jesus Christ.

The writer does not hold back: Jesus Christ is everything. He is all in all. He was a partner with the Father in creation. He upholds the universe. He came to earth to free us from the stains of sin. He now sits at the right hand of the Father. We are left breathless! Nowhere—except possibly in Col. 1:15-20—can we find a more magnificent witness to Jesus Christ as eternal Lord!

The key phrase in unlocking the meaning of this opening section is found in verse 4: "superior to angels." Angels are referred to again in verses 5, 6, 7, and 13.

Why angels? For our ears the reference sounds strange. When was the last time you thought about angels? Who believes in angels today? They simply are not a part of our contemporary scene. Imbued as we are with a materialistic approach to life, we simply do not think much about invisible worlds populated by nonhuman creatures.

Little wonder that Hebrews is a mystery to us! Were we living in the first century we might better understand what the writer is trying to tell us. His world assumed the existence of invisible beings populating the atmosphere. People in those days believed that "ministering spirits" (1:14) created out of a fiery stream existed only long enough to complete some God-assigned duty before perishing.

1:5–14

The author's pupose in these verses is to show that angels, though important creatures of God, cannot compare with Jesus Christ. Angels are temporary; he is eternal. They are servants; he is the Son. They are created; he is one with the Creator.

In order to drive home his point, the author uses a method that seems strange and foreign to us. In fact, by modern standards it almost smacks of a certain dishonesty. Quotations are drawn from a number of places in the Old Testament. These quotations supposedly "prove" that Jesus Christ is superior to angels and that he is the very Son of God.

I remember well my first attempt to study these Old Testament references. I dutifully looked up each cross-reference. I studied carefully the context and setting of each. I began with the assumption that each reference would be clear and obvious. But the more I studied the more confused I became. In fact, I found myself growing downright irritated with the author for what seemed to be completely unwarranted interpretations of these Old Testament references.

It was at this point that I stumbled quite by accident onto an article that made me both embarrassed and ashamed at the same time. I realized that I had been judging the author by the scholarly standards of my century rather than his. More importantly, I learned that the method he used is still regarded by Orthodox Jews as of great value in biblical interpretation.

What is that method? It is an approach to Scripture that regards *every word* as having a specific and profound meaning, regardless of the setting or context in which it is used. Each word of course had its obvious meaning. But beyond that the same word had other meanings as well, including a deep and hidden meaning that could be discovered only after careful and painstaking study of that word.

This is why the role of the rabbi was so crucial to Judaism. In the course of time certain wise and respected rabbis emerged as the chief interpreters of religion and the Scriptures.

To his credit, the author of Hebrews employs the most respected method of biblical interpretation for arriving at his conclusions. He is saying in effect, "After patient and prayerful study of these references from the Old Testament I have come to the conclusion that they speak about Jesus Christ. Furthermore, I have concluded that they establish Jesus Christ as being superior to the angels who were created by God for a good but inferior purpose."

Once we pass this hurdle of interpretation, we can sit back and receive the epistle for what it really is—the author's witness to Jesus Christ as Lord. Had he not already believed in Jesus Christ as Lord these interpretations would never have been made. Had there not already been a prior firm conviction about Christ's superiority to all other created beings, the writer would not have discovered it in these obscure passages from the Old Testament.

There is an important lesson here for all of us. We sometimes think that the way to witness as Christians is to establish our case on firm grounds, to "prove" that we are right, to win the day by clear logic. When witnesses from a sect group appear at our door and we decide to engage them in conversation, we usually try to answer logical point with logical point. Now, there is nothing wrong with logic. We must remember, however, that the basis for our conviction is not some logically airtight case but a personal conviction that Christ is Lord. Logic may have won some arguments along the way, but it has seldom persuaded anyone to trust in Jesus Christ. The only convincing witness is that which arises out of a deep and firm personal certainty that Jesus Christ is indeed the better way.

2:1-4

Because of his deeply embedded beliefs, articulated in Hebrews 1, the author is greatly distressed about the unbelieving condition of his readers. Accordingly, in these opening verses of chapter 2 he launches into the first of the "sermonettes" to which we referred in the Introduction. Feeling that his hearers have drifted away from their former faith, he urges them to come back to their earlier commitment. He fears that, having begun so well, they may have lost by neglect what had once been so important to them.

The word "neglect" in verse 3 is the same Greek term that in Matt. 22:5, in the familiar parable of the wedding feast, is translated "made light of." As the potential guests received the invitation to the wedding, they "made light of it," assuming other things—even the most mundane—to be of greater importance. To "neglect" something, then, is not to reject it openly and vociferously, but merely to consider it of little importance.

The phrase "pay the closer attention" in verse 1 is also of special interest. It renders a Greek term that means "to cling to something." Imagine people clinging to a rope as they inch their way across a deep chasm and you have something of the force of this idea.

In the course of my ministry I have met many people who once firmly embraced the Christian faith and participated actively in the life of the church. It seemed safe to assume that they would always do so. But somewhere along the line things changed. The once-vibrant confession turned to lethargy and indifference. Regular worship and reception of the sacrament had degenerated into occasional worship or no churchgoing at all.

When one inquires into the reason for this change, one is surprised to learn that it is seldom due to intellectual doubt or to unhappiness with the church. More often than not, the root cause is precisely the same as it was for those first-century Christians—neglect!

As C. S. Lewis points out in his *Screwtape Letters,* temptation seldom comes in the expected ways. The Evil One is much too clever for that—he knows that it is neglect more than anything else that can nudge us out of the kingdom. To put off devotional reading "until tomorrow," to miss worship "just this one Sunday," to postpone teaching Sunday church school "until next year," to give more generously "once I get a better job"—these are the stuff of neglect. And neglect, more than open rejection, has most often been the reason why people become lost from the church and from the faith.

2:5-18

The Son of Man—Our Brother

2:5-9

Having established in Hebrews 1 that Jesus Christ is superior to angels because he is the Son of God, the author now goes on to establish a second basic conviction: Christ is also superior in that he is the Son of man. Angels could not by their own nature attain to oneness with God; neither could they become one with humankind. Thus, Jesus Christ is superior in this way too. He did what angels could not do: he became fully and completely human.

In order to "prove" his point the writer again resorts to an unusual method of Scripture interpretation. He draws on a passage from Psalm 8 and claims that the "Son of man" title is more than a reference to humankind. Its inner or hidden meaning is connected to Jesus Christ, who became "for a little while lower than the angels" during his life on earth.

The key word in this section is "death." As will become evident in succeeding chapters, the author of Hebrews has little interest in the events of the life of Jesus prior to his death. There are no references in this epistle to Jesus' birth, his teachings, his miracles, or his conflict with the religious leaders. Like Paul in his epistles, the writer here focuses almost exclusively on the death and resurrection of Christ.

In a world like ours that avoids death at all costs, a world in which we bend every effort to blunt the effect of death when it finally does come, it is difficult to grasp the author's point. Let us begin by acknowledging that the one thing we all have in common is not death *and* taxes but death alone. Rich or poor, sick or healthy, old or young, black or white, religious or irreligious—it makes absolutely no difference. At some point, sooner or later, all of us inevitably face the reality of our own death: My life stops—period.

This raises an interesting question: If Jesus Christ were to become fully and completely human, how should he prove his humanity? In what one way could he make absolutely certain that he would identify with every last human being on earth? What one experience would bind him inextricably with all who have lived—from the dawn of creation to the end of time? The answer of course is . . . death.

What strikes us at first as morbid and bleak soon turns into the most cheerful and hopeful word we can possibly imagine. After all, we too will one day have to die—you and I—every last one of us. But there is good news! In his death Jesus Christ signaled the ultimate victory. Now ''crowned with glory and honor'' in his resurrection, he gives reassurance to everyone who faces death—and that includes us all.

There were two or three occasions in my otherwise healthy life when I lived under a cloud of uncertainty for several days. Symptoms could have meant malignancy and imminent death. Those were not pleasant days. In the back of my mind I began to plan for what I would do if the doctor brought bad news. I thought about arrangements I would want to make for my family, words I would say to friends, contingencies I would have to provide for at my office.

But even after all those things have been worked out in one's mind, there remains the ultimate question: How shall I face my own death? The closer one draws to death the more one walks a solitary road. In the last days, even one's deeply loved mate must let go and allow one to walk on alone. The good news is that no one really walks alone. Jesus Christ, the Son of man, went all the way to death. He tasted death ''for every one.''

2:10–18

The theme from the previous section continues here: Jesus Christ identifies completely with us in death. But now we encounter some fascinating words and phrases that help us understand more completely how he does this.

First, there is the reference to Christ as "the pioneer of their salvation." Certainly he was not the pioneer in the sense of being the first to die. But he is the pioneer in a more important sense: he is the first to find his way through the seemingly impenetrable mountain range to the land beyond. And once he found the way he opened it for all who went before him without finding a way, and for all who followed after him and would now find the way through him.

Then comes that magnificent phrase, "He is not ashamed to call them brethren." To appreciate its full impact one must think back to what was said at the opening of the epistle—Jesus Christ is the "heir of all things"; he "bears the very stamp of [God's] nature"; he is "upholding the universe by his word of power." Set all of that on one side. Then, over against it, set what we have just read: "He is not ashamed to call them brethren." Is there any place in the Bible where the good news is more fully and completely proclaimed? Think of it—the eternal and all-powerful Son of God has become so completely human that he is not ashamed to be one of us!

At times I have been ashamed of myself, and for good reason. At times I have been ashamed of others, sometimes for good reason, but more often because I was more worried about my reputation than about their welfare. I feared that someone else's shame might somehow reflect on my character. Not so with Christ. Disregarding all concern for himself, he becomes one with every human being.

This astonishing news is further reinforced by the phrase, "He had to be made like his brethren in every respect." Once more we are left stunned by the completeness of his identity with us. He does not stand off at a distance looking sympathetically at us in our broken and fallen condition. He does not even stand at our side, holding our hand and consoling us in our helplessness. He goes beyond all that by actually taking upon himself all of our sinfulness, our grief, our loneliness, our brokenness, our illness, our alienation, and ultimately even our death.

At times we edge toward despair. No one escapes its prospect. Even the great saints refer to the "dry seasons," when God seems far away and no one understands what we are going through. Once more the message from our friend, the author of Hebrews, comes through: Jesus Christ became so fully and completely human that no event in life, not the deepest and darkest valley of despair, not even death itself can separate us from him who became like us "in every respect."

I loved my dad so much that his sudden death came as a terrible shock. There were too many things left unsaid, especially words of gratitude. The whole family needed words of consolation. We found them in Romans 8. Sitting around the kitchen table, the eight of us children and our mother reached out to grasp those anchored phrases: "For I am sure that neither death, nor life, . . . nor things to come, nor powers, nor height, nor depth, nor anything else in all creation, will be able to separate us from the love of God in Christ Jesus our Lord" (Rom. 8:38–39).

3:1—4:13
A Better Leader

3:1-6

Now the author of Hebrews turns in earnest to Old Testament references, drawing comparisons between them and Jesus Christ. Here for the first time he refers to Jesus specifically as "high priest"—something that no other New Testament writer does. He will develop the idea in greater detail near the end of chapter 4. In the present context he only alludes to it—a hint of something yet to come.

The main allusion in chapter 3 is to Moses, who is traditionally ranked with Abraham and David as the most revered and respected of ancient leaders. The writer does not put down Moses in order to lift up Jesus Christ. On the contrary, he honors Moses as a faithful servant, as a man who fulfilled the purpose God had set before him.

But that is exactly the point: Moses was faithful as a servant; Christ was faithful as a son! The distinction between servant and son is difficult for most of us to grasp. Other than entrepreneurs in farming and small business perhaps, few people today expect their offspring to follow in their own occupational footsteps. The entry of women into a broad range of careers further alters the old-time picture of children pursuing the vocations of their parents.

Try to envision the culture of that ancient time. There were three primary classes—farmers, business persons, and servants/slaves. Those who were fortunate enough to own a farm or a business spent much of their energy planning for the future. Crucial to that future was to have a son—and preferably many sons—to whom one could pass on the farm or the business. To work hard for a lifetime and then give one's land or shop to a servant was not out of the question, but was surely not a preferred option. Clearly a son had status such a servant could never know.

Again, the writer of Hebrews is not denigrating the work of Moses. Moses was a faithful servant, but he was not a son. God has only one Son, Jesus Christ. He and he alone is related directly to the Father.

Although the author of Hebrews does not directly mention the Trinity, that is the question that really lies at the heart of this section on Moses and Christ. Moses, faithful though he may have been, was not without fault. He failed on many occasions. His pride, anger, and impatience often brought disaster to those who followed him. Not so with Jesus Christ, the Son of God. He can be trusted absolutely because of who he is. He is without fault, trustworthy, completely faithful.

Like Moses in his day, pastors today play a key role in the life of the believing community. Church people look to them for guidance. They expect their pastors to be faithful spiritual leaders. But those who expect perfection from their pastor will soon be disappointed. No matter how faithful, effective, or compassionate, a pastor is a human being. As in the case of Moses, so with pastors today: pride, anger, impatience—and a host of other sins and shortcomings—continue at times to bring grief to the church.

It is for this reason that we, like the early Christians, need to look beyond the servant to the Savior. Pastors function not to call attention to themselves but to point to Jesus Christ, the Son of God. People sometimes leave the church because of disappointment over a pastor. Little wonder. It is only when we fix our hope exclusively on Jesus Christ that we will have the confidence and hope of which the author of Hebrews speaks.

The Corinthian Christians once played the familiar game of "My Favorite Pastor." Some preferred Paul. Others liked Apollos better. Still others thought Cephas was a cut above them both. In his first letter to these Corinthians (3:7), Paul takes them to task for making such useless comparisons. He reminds his readers that each of these leaders had contributed something to the planting and watering of the seeds of faith at Corinth, but "only God . . . gives the growth."

3:7-19

We now come to what appears to be another "sermonette," which will continue through 4:13. Having just established the superiority of Christ over Moses, the author seems moved to digress for a moment and bear down on the importance of following Christ without wavering.

Once more the writer's reference is to an Old Testament story, in this case the account of that time in the wilderness when the Israelites ran out of water (Num. 20:2-13). Moses had been instructed to command a rock to yield water. Instead he struck the rock, probably out of anger and frustration. His violent act is seen as symptomatic of the rebellious spirit of the entire people. The place was called Meribah, meaning "contention." In a later reference to this episode, in Psalm 95, the whole nation is judged to be in contention against God.

We said earlier that the destination of the Letter to the Hebrews is uncertain. What is certain is that these early Christians, like their Israelite forebears, are on the verge of the same unbelief that brought judgment at Meribah. The same rebellion and hardness of heart will result in the same alienation from God. The only escape from judgment is through repentance. And the time to repent is always "today."

The call for daily repentance is easily overlooked. Martin Luther understood its importance when he wrote about our lifelong need to put to death *daily* the old nature in order that the new nature might be renewed *daily*.

This raises an interesting question: How many days does one have to repent? How many days to say "I'm sorry"? How many days to right a wrong? How many days to mend and restore a broken relationship? Although we would like to think that "there's always tomorrow," we know we have no such assurance. The advice of Scripture is to deal with our wrath before the sun goes down. Prompt repentance is crucial to our relationships with God, our families, our friends, and whomever we sin against.

As the author points out, the effect of accumulated and unconfessed sin is hardness of heart. One does not turn into a hardened and insensitive person overnight, but a sharp word here and a neglected kindness there, an insult here and an angry reply there, a belittling remark here and a broken promise there—eventually they take their toll. Gradually, and without realizing it, we develop within ourselves the very hardness we so much despise in others.

The only remedy is daily repentance: "Today, when you hear his voice, do not harden your hearts."

4:1–11

In this section the "sermonette" continues and the same basic theme carries over, namely, that persistent repudiation of God's call to repentance leads to hardness of the heart. But now the author picks up another strand from the wilderness experience of the Israelites. From the moment the people of Israel left Egypt, the wandering tribes yearned for the day when they would stop wandering through the hot and hostile wilderness and settle down in their own land.

But this privilege would be denied them because of their rebellion. Even Moses himself, in spite of his faithfulness, would never know the "rest" to be had in the Promised Land. Even the next generation, under the leadership of Joshua, would also fail to know the true "rest" that God had intended. To be sure, they actually entered the land of Canaan; they were finally able to "settle in." But theirs was not the kind of "rest" God had in mind. Constant harassment and continuous warfare, coupled with compromise and inconsistency, meant that the dreams for the Promised Land never became reality.

The author of Hebrews sees here a parallel to the situation of his readers. Like the Israelites of old, they have been set free from slavery; they too have become children of a new exodus. Their freedom, however, is far greater than any the Israelites could have known. Now the deliverer is not Moses; the leader is not another Joshua. Instead, they have been freed by none other than Jesus Christ, the very Son of God. That being the case, the consequences of deliverance are likewise that much greater. To rebel against Moses on the hot sands of Sinai, when food and water were scarce, is one thing; but to rebel against Jesus Christ, who has set us free by his death and resurrection, is quite another thing.

We often think of the advantage we have in living in the New Testament era. How good to be able to look back to the cross and resurrection, rather than to wonder about how God will in the future set his people free. How good to be the beneficiary of many generations of faith rather than to bear the responsibility of setting the pace and of seeking to understand how one should tell one's children about the ways in which God will reveal himself.

But should not our great joy be offset by the awesome burden we carry? It is indeed a privilege to live in the New Testament era, but it is also a heavy responsibility. Discipleship is costly. Unlike the Israelites, we cannot claim that God's ways are obscure and the goal is uncertain. For us, the way is Jesus Christ and the goal is to extend his kingdom to the whole world. And even though the final destination for our ''rest'' still lies in the future, there is a sense in which we already have the benefit of that ''rest.'' We know a ''peace that passes understanding.''

What, then, is the writer of Hebrews saying to us? The responsibility for a New Testament believer is greater. And greater too is the judgment if we harden our heart against this greater message and fail to carry out this greater mission.

4:11–13

If every good sermon is marked by a good conclusion, the author of Hebrews is an excellent preacher. In these verses he brings to a close the ''sermonette'' that began at 3:7.

Verse 12 is the first of several familiar passages from this epistle: ''For the word of God is living and active, sharper than any two-edged sword.'' When we read ''word of God'' we automatically translate it to mean "the Bible." The writer of Hebrews, of course, did not have the same Bible we know today. Although they were in common use at the time Hebrews was written, the thirty-nine books of our Old Testament were just then being gathered by Judaism into a single volume of sacred writings. And it would be another three centuries before the church formally recognized the twenty-seven books of the New Testament as inspired writings.

So what does the author mean by "word of God"? There is little doubt that he means what any devout Jew would have meant when using that phrase, namely, "the revelation of God." We are accustomed to thinking of "word of God" as being limited to the Bible, so we may feel uncomfortable with the notion that anything other than the Bible deserves that title. But we may be robbing ourselves of the full power and effect of the "word of God" if we too-narrowly restrict its meaning. In fact, the full impact of the Bible itself may be blunted if we allow no other sources to speak to us as "word of God," and in so doing help us to understand the Bible.

Luther reminds us that "word of God" means more than just one thing. At its heart, "word of God" refers to Jesus Christ. As John 1:1–14 tells us, the Word who in the beginning was with God became flesh in his incarnation. "Word of God" is also that "good news" which lies at the heart of the Bible, that gospel which is seen and heard more clearly in some places (such as the Gospels, the prophets, and the epistles) than in other places (such as the Old Testament historical books or books of wisdom). "Word of God" can also be applied to any message that reminds us that God created the world, redeemed it through Jesus Christ, and continues to reveal himself through the Holy Spirit. Thus, a sermon, the witness of another Christian, a good book, a kind gesture, even a revelation of God's will through nature can be understood as the "word of God." The key is whether the message of revelation points to Jesus Christ. Whatever does not is not the "word of God," no matter how lofty the thought or intention. As the author points out in verses 12 and 13, an authentic "word" from God always leads to an honest look at ourselves. Christ is the most authentic person who ever lived. An encounter with him as "Word of God" forces us to be honest with ourselves. Only this daily experience of open and honest confession in the presence of God can keep us on the way that leads to "rest."

4:14—7:28
A Better High Priest

4:14-16

We now come to that portion of Hebrews which can be described as unique in the New Testament. In these chapters the author refers to Jesus Christ as "high priest"—a title no other New Testament writer uses.

Again, we need to go back to the Old Testament roots of the church if we are to understand the meaning. These chapters recall the great Day of Atonement described in Leviticus 16 and 17, the annual festival of sacrifice and renewal for the people of Israel. In the midst of all the ritual on the Day of Atonement, two things stood out: First, a high priest was needed to represent God's presence to the people and to represent the people before God. Second, even the most respected high priest dared not come before God empty-handed; he needed to bring a sacrifice. It is the first of these two points—the high priest theme—that carries through this section of Hebrews.

The opening verses form an introduction to the material about Christ as high priest. Once more—as in chapters 1 and 2—the divine and human natures of Christ are set before us. Here, however, it is done within the space of two verses.

In verse 14 Jesus Christ is lifted up as the cosmic high priest—"a great high priest who has passed through the heavens." Rather than looking forward in time, we are urged to look upward in space. Not just time, but also space is under the rule of God and has been redeemed by Jesus Christ.

The consequences of this idea for us who live in the "space age" are mind-boggling. Until the last quarter century the

Christian church, when we talked about Christian hope, focused almost exclusively on time. There was much speculation about the ages to come, about the second coming of Christ and our hope for the future. But space exploration in recent years has drawn our attention in a different direction—upward in space. Far ahead of his own time, the writer of Hebrews has a message for our day and our age—Jesus Christ, God's chosen high priest, is Lord of space!

Lest we become too carried away with our speculations about space, verse 15 turns us about abruptly and brings us back to earth. Our cosmic high priest is also one who is able to "sympathize with our weaknesses." He has been "tempted as we are, yet without sin."

This is pure gospel! The cosmic Christ, acquainted with Mars and Saturn and distant suns and planets beyond the reach of our most powerful and sophisticated space probes, is able to understand the heartaches, sorrows, and temptations of the last and least of us on earth! We all feel lonely and isolated at times. Sometimes our alienation from others seems so complete that we feel no one understands; no one cares. The good news from Hebrews is that there is always one who understands and cares—Jesus Christ; and for this reason we are encouraged to have confidence to draw near the throne of grace and receive mercy and help in time of need.

5:1-10

Following a pattern established earlier, the writer now—after having set down a general idea in the previous verses—goes into detail to explain his point. Since the theme here is the high priesthood, it is important to explore the roots of the system in the Old Testament.

We tend to think of the Old Testament priesthood as something passed on from one generation to the next within the same family. In a sense, that was the case. The tribe of Levi had specific responsibility for priestly duties.

But we are reminded in these verses that there was also a deeper root to the priestly system, one that is often overlooked.

When the system operated at its best in Israel, the high priest was more than simply a Levite; he was also a person of integrity and sensitivity. As he carried the blood of the sacrifice into the holy of holies on the Day of Atonement, the high priest knew that this was a time of sacrifice for the people. But he also knew that it was a time when he himself—"beset with weakness"—needed to receive forgiveness. Thus, when he offered sacrifice it was "for his own sins as well as for those of the people."

No pastor who reads these verses can escape a profound sense of identity with the high priest. Each time a pastor conducts a service of worship there is a dual role to be filled: represent God's presence to the people and lead the people into the presence of God. But the dual function involves a danger. One can easily think of oneself as merely doing a job or filling a role. There is the danger of merely going through the motions.

The best antidote for such an attitude is to come back again and again to the point made in these verses: the pastor is also a sinner—"beset with weakness"—who needs God's mercy as much as any other member of the congregation. One's role as the called leader of the congregation does not deliver one from weakness and sin. If anything, the temptations are even greater.

And just in case we pastors are inclined to think at times that the church should be grateful that we have chosen to follow the pastoral calling, the text quickly puts us to shame with the forthright claim that even Christ "did not exalt himself to be made a high priest." Our calling to preach the Word and administer the sacraments is nothing of which we can boast. The call and appointment come from God. Like everything else, it is a gift of his grace.

5:11–14

We come again to what appears to be an interruption in the flow of the epistle, another "sermonette" that springs up out of the writer's concern for the spiritual condition of his readers. This one begins here and continues to the end of chapter 6.

Having just given his readers some profound and provocative ideas, the author seems to fall into a state of despair and discouragement. Knowing how the faithful have drifted away from their early enthusiasm for the gospel, he fears that they may have become so sluggish and "dull of hearing" that his words will pass in one ear and out the other. Whereas they ought by now to be teachers themselves, they have instead slipped so far back that they are like spiritual babies, in need of milk rather than solid food.

Anyone who preaches or teaches in the church will understand the author's struggle. After hours of careful research, reflection, and writing, one often steps up to the pulpit or podium with the nettlesome question in mind: Who will understand what I have to say? Who really cares? And on Monday morning comes the compromising thought: Why spend so much energy in my preparations this week? Few seem to grasp what I want them so desperately to understand. I may as well use my time for other efforts.

Those who resist such temptation eventually develop an approach to preaching and teaching that regards as inviolable certain basic guidelines: First, I must preach and teach so that even the most immature person in the audience will have a chance to hear the gospel; I must search for illustration, allusion, symbol, and example in order that something in my presentation might be used by the Spirit to catch the interest of even the most disinterested and unattentive listener. Second, I must not give in to a "lowest common denominator" mentality. Unlike Elijah, I must remember that I have no right to make snap judgments about the faithfulness of God's people. Among those who hear me will be some—and probably more than I realize—who are mature and hungry for a challenging and stimulating word from God. For their sake I must again apply myself to prayer, study, and careful thought so that they will find a resource for their continuing growth in grace.

6:1–12

In these verses we encounter one of the most difficult ideas in the entire epistle. Carrying forward the emphasis from the previous section, the writer deplores the spiritual condition of his readers. In spite of every advantage for growth toward maturity, they are still enmeshed in "the elementary doctrine" of the Christian faith.

So dismayed is the author over their immaturity that he doubts any possibility of renewal: "It is impossible to restore again to repentance those who have once been enlightened . . . if they then commit apostasy." The words have a ring of finality. The author appears to see no hope for these backslider believers.

Before we jump to that conclusion, however, it is important to listen to the more moderate tone of verses 9 and 10. Having given a stern warning that verges on complete hopelessness, the writer pulls back a bit and speaks words of meager but certain consolation. There is, after all, some small reason for hope, some weak but definite sign of encouragement. "We feel sure of better things" does not sound like a ringing, solidly based affirmation, but it is at least an expression of some faint expectation.

Jesus also spoke harsh words from time to time. Like the author of Hebrews, Jesus was appalled that so privileged a people could have drifted so far from God's purpose. He was especially hard on the most advantaged among his own people—the scribes and the Pharisees. Like the original readers of the Letter to the Hebrews, they too had started well. A reform movement at one time, Pharisaism had brought much-needed change to Judaism. But the Pharisees had long since lost their vision and sense of direction. Little wonder that Jesus had such stern words for them. Little wonder that he was reluctant to "cast pearls before swine" (Matt. 7:6).

Yet, in spite of his disappointment with some who opposed him, in spite of stern warnings to them about judgment, our Lord is, at the same time, a person of infinite tenderness and understanding. He will not quench the slightest flicker of fire in a smoking flax, nor will he break off a reed that is holding on by only the slimmest fiber. In his last words on the cross Jesus speaks the ultimate in mercy for those who deserve judgment: "Father, forgive them; for they know not what they do" (Luke 23:34).

This tension between judgment and mercy is always a part of the church's responsibility. When we do not call people to account for their actions, when we water down the cost of discipleship, when we give false comfort to those who drift from the church and take lightly the discipline of worship and service, we do an injustice to the gospel. To give the impression that generous giving is optional, or that service to others is a mere matter of choice, is detrimental both to the hearer of such a message and to the church itself. There is plenty of room in the message of the church for rebuke and the call to repentance. There is room for a word of judgment.

But judgment without mercy is not gospel. Since even the most mature believer falls far short of God's expectations, no one can escape judgment. But a message that accents only judgment leaves the impression that an improvement here and an adjustment there will please God and bring his approval. True, God looks for such improvements. As the text says, "God is not so unjust as to overlook your work and the love which you showed." In the end, however, nothing but mercy will save us. Nothing but God's word of pardon will remove the cloud of despair that comes over us when we realize that even our best is not good enough.

6:13–20

The author continues his "sermonette" by reminding his readers that God remains steadfast and faithful even though they themselves have been unreliable and faithless. In order to make this point, the writer conjures up an illustration that may easily elude us. Accustomed as we are to contracts, deeds, written agreements, and detailed legal documents to cover all circumstances, it is difficult for us to understand the mind-set of a paperless culture that put absolute confidence in a person's word. In most of our formal dealings with other people, written contracts are essential. We even scrutinize the fine print to make certain there are no loopholes that could make us vulnerable to a future lawsuit.

The world of the early Christians was quite different. While there were indeed some written contracts, most business was carried on by verbal agreement in the presence of a witness. You were as good as your word. And if in addition you invoked God as a witness, that agreement became absolute and irrevocable.

Against this background the argument here is fascinating. The writer says that God made a promise to Abraham and his descendants. The fact that God is the maker of the promise is sufficient to ensure its validity and durability, since God could invoke no higher authority than himself for ensuring the promise. But in order to make absolutely certain that the promise is reliable, God takes an oath upon himself to fulfill it. That is to say, he makes *doubly* sure there can be no question about the certainty and reliability of his promise to Abraham.

This whole intriguing argument is intended to assure the readers of the epistle that they can count on it: God will stand behind the promises he made to them. Their hope, like an anchor firmly embedded in the rocky floor of the ocean, cannot be shaken.

Some lines of the familiar Navy hymn "My Hope is Built on Nothing Less Than Jesus' Blood and Righteousness" spring directly from these verses. As the author of Hebrews envisions the church as a ship riding the rough seas with its anchor fixed in the unseen depths, so the author of the hymn describes the Christian experience:

In every high and stormy gale
My anchor holds within the veil.

If we have difficulty understanding the nature of a verbal promise, we also have trouble comprehending the meaning of "hope" as that word is used in the New Testament; for us the term always seems to include an element of uncertainty and tentativeness. The problem lies in the way our language uses the word. Most words lose something in translation. As used in the New Testament by the early Christians, the word for "hope" contained no note whatsoever of uncertainty. Hope was a settled matter, a fact that could be trusted absolutely. It was never a question of "if," but only of "when." "Hope" was never followed by a question mark, but always by an exclamation point.

7:1–14

Having completed his third "sermonette," the author once again picks up the main line of thought and we find ourselves moving into the most complex part of this epistle. Here we are introduced to our "mystery guest," an obscure Old Testament character by the name of Melchizedek. Although Melchizedek was first mentioned in passing at 5:6, it is not until chapter 7 that we understand why the writer wishes to recall him.

Genesis 14 reports the brief encounter between Abraham and Melchizedek. Abraham has just rescued his nephew Lot from neighboring kings. In the process Abraham has accumulated a good deal of booty. On his return from battle he meets Melchizedek, described as "king of Salem" and "priest of God Most High." Melchizedek blesses Abraham, who in turn gives Melchizedek "a tenth of everything." And there the encounter ends. As abruptly as he appears he disappears, and we hear no more of Melchizedek.

But for some strange reason, speculation about Melchizedek did not disappear from Judaism. In Psalm 110 he reappears and is described as "a priest for ever" (Ps. 110:4). The Dead Sea Scrolls reveal that Melchizedek was also the subject of much discussion late in the first century A.D., at about the time the Letter to the Hebrews was written. After Jerusalem was destroyed in A.D. 70, a group of devout and ascetic Jews settled on the northwest shore of the Dead Sea and developed a community called Qumran. When scrolls were discovered in 1948 and this area began to be excavated, the Qumran writings showed that these dedicated Jews held Melchizedek in high regard and speculated a great deal about him.

Until the discovery of the Dead Sea Scrolls, scholars were puzzled about the reference to Melchizedek in Hebrews. But it is no longer a puzzle. Given the fact that Hebrews is probably addressed to Christians out of the Jewish community, and given the fact that within this community there was much discussion about Melchizedek, there is little wonder that the writer of Hebrews should have referred to him.

That is the easy part. Now comes the difficult task of unraveling the complex way in which Melchizedek is used in Hebrews to make a point about Jesus Christ. A diagram may be of help.

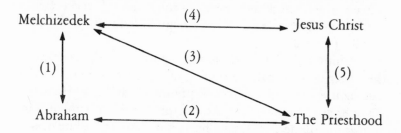

The author seems to be making five points:

(1) Melchizedek is superior to Abraham. This is proved by the fact that Abraham gives the gift of the tithe to Melchizedek, not vice versa.

(2) The Levites, who make up the priesthood, are descendants of Abraham and therefore of the same stature as Abraham.

(3) Because he is superior to Abraham, Melchizedek is also superior to the Levitical priesthood.

(4) Using the same method of interpretation we first encountered in Hebrews 1, the author asserts that Jesus Christ, like Melchizedek, is "a priest for ever."

(5) The conclusion: Jesus Christ is superior to the Levitical priesthood.

Although the line of reasoning may seem strange and circuitous to our twentieth-century way of looking at things, we must recall that the author is to be judged, not by our standards, but by what was seen as the best approach in his own culture. By that measurement, his argumentation is understandable and powerful.

More important for us is to grasp his conclusion, which brings us back to the main theme of his epistle. This is the author's confession that Jesus Christ stands over and above all things, the plea that his readers cling to the better way in Christ rather than return to their old ways in Judaism. For us, the call is to join the author in his confession that Jesus Christ is all in all, that Christ is "the way, and the truth, and the life" (John 14:6).

7:15-28

Three phrases unlock the treasure of this section: "weakness and uselessness" (verse 18); "a better hope" (verse 19); and "once for all" (verse 27).

Continuing the line of reasoning begun earlier in the chapter, the writer tells us that the coming of Jesus Christ uncovers the true nature of the old system of priesthood and law. He is not saying that these were no good for their time, or without purpose as forerunners for Jesus Christ, but—and this is the meaning of "weakness and uselessness"—that they brought no lasting answers to the enigma of sin. The priesthood was both temporal and transitory. High priest succeeded high priest. The coming of Christ ushered in the dawn of a new age and with it "a better hope." Because he was divine as well as human, the consequences of his ministry as high priest reached into the eternal realm and ended the need for a succession of high priests. "Once for all" he filled the necessary role of entering the eternal holy of holies.

In verse 25 all of this is brought together and applied to the life of the church: "Consequently he is able for all time to save those who draw near to God through him, since he always lives to make intercession for them." As we observed earlier, the writer of Hebrews has a remarkable way of drawing us into a complex line of reasoning and then, just when we least expect it, springing at us with a simple statement about the gospel—a word that leaves us almost speechless. So it is here in verse 25. What is more central to the good news, or how could one say it better than that no one is left out; all are invited to "draw near to God through him." And in those moments that come to all of us, moments when we do not feel like praying, when we feel forsaken by God and family, when the last thread is about to break and we no longer know how to pray for a son or daughter or friend—there is no better news than to know that ''he always lives to make intercession for them''!

What way can be better than this way? What faith or message could be more hopeful or helpful? Of what other religious figure in all the annals of history can it be said that ''he is able for all time to save''? Once more the author of Hebrews has led us to the very heart of the gospel!

8:1-13

A Better Covenant

8:1-7

Chapter 8 provides a transition between the two central themes of the epistle. Having now completed the argument about Christ as perfect high priest, the author begins moving toward his second accent, namely that Jesus Christ is also the perfect sacrifice. To lay the groundwork, however, this skillful writer employs another image from the Old Testament—the idea of the covenant.

There is probably no other theme or emphasis as central to all of Scripture—both Old Testament and New—than this idea of covenant. Whether it began at creation, or with Noah, or with Abraham, it is present in all its aspects in the experience of Abraham as told in Genesis 12.

At the risk of oversimplification we can say that these fundamental aspects—in the covenant experience of Abraham—are three:

(1) the initiative of God: "I will bless you" (Gen. 12:2);
(2) the faithful response: "So Abram went" (Gen. 12:4); and
(3) the promise for others: "By you all the families of the earth shall bless themselves" (Gen. 12:3).

In succeeding generations many things changed for the Israelites. At times they were free and settled, at other times in bondage and exile. Their fortunes went from better to worse to better, depending on a variety of circumstances. But one thing remained constant: they knew they were God's covenant people.

In fact, they were so sure of the covenant God had made with them that they assumed he was obliged to bless them no matter what they did, no matter how faithless they were. It was in these times of faithlessness that God raised up prophets to call the people to repentance. The prophets used a variety of illustrations to point up Israel's failure: a faithless wife, a barren tree, a vine without grapes, a valley of dry bones. Whatever the illustration, the point was the same: Israel had failed. The covenant was broken again. Only God could renew it.

The author of Hebrews adds a new perspective to all this: not only were the Israelites at fault for breaking the covenant; the covenant itself was faulty!

To understand the author's point, we need to lift out two words from verse 5—"copy" and "shadow." Taking his cue from the philosophy of the Greeks, the writer seems to assume the commonly accepted notion that everything in the material world is an imperfect "copy" or "shadow" of something that exists in an ideal world. Applying this notion to Old Testament events, he says that everything associated with the old covenant is a "copy" or "shadow" of something better. Tabernacle, sacrifice, priesthood, even the covenant itself—each is an imperfect symbol or "copy" that looked beyond itself to a comparable reality that was perfect and complete.

Against this background it can be seen that Christ is the perfect high priest who inaugurates a new covenant, a perfect covenant that needs no periodic renewal, one that is forever established by his perfect ministry.

8:8–13

Having described the new covenant instituted by Jesus Christ, the author now goes on to "prove" that the sacred writings themselves speak about this new covenant. The inadequacy of the old covenant is suggested already in Jeremiah's talk of a new covenant.

In previous citations from the Old Testament the writer had tended to put together a composite of many brief references from several sources. Here the entire quotation is from a single prophet, the words of Jeremiah 31. Spoken at a time when the fortunes of Israel were at their lowest, these words of Jeremiah have proved a source of comfort and encouragement to suffering believers and discouraged saints in every generation.

Jeremiah's message is that a new covenant and a new day lie in the future. God will not forsake his people. He will remember his promises. No matter how dismal life may become, we must hold firmly to him who will set us free.

How is this message to be understood by those of us who now live in the New Testament era, at a time when Christ has already come and the new covenant has already been established? What will sustain us in times of distress?

It seems best to answer these questions with a "double-edged" reply: In our age God's promises have *already* been fulfilled, but at the same time *not yet* fulfilled. There is a tension between these two aspects of the Christian experience.

On the one hand the church and the individual Christian can say, "The promises of God are *already* fulfilled. The life, death, and resurrection of Jesus Christ complete all that is needed for the mission of the church and the salvation of the individual. When Jesus cried out from the cross, 'It is finished,' he fulfilled all of the requirements for the new covenant."

At the same time we find ourselves saying, "We live in a broken world that affects the church and every believer. In this broken world we have much work yet to do. The promises of God have *not yet* been entirely fulfilled. We look forward in hope to the completion of God's plan for us as a church. I look forward in hope to the completion of God's plan for me as an individual Christian."

At the very end of the chapter, after a lengthy quotation from Jeremiah, verse 13 adds a brief but significant comment. The author's carefully chosen word "obsolete" offers another key to unlocking his epistle. It avoids the implication that the old covenant was never of any value, was always worthless, was ineffective in its time. Rather, the idea is conveyed that the old covenant was indeed useful in its day, but that, with the coming of Christ, a new day had now dawned.

This text helps us in relating to believers of different religious backgrounds, and especially Judaism. The links between Christianity and Judaism are very close because of our common heritage. Our Christian Bible includes the Jewish Scriptures. It would be tragic and grossly insensitive for a Christian to say to a follower of Judaism, "Your religion is worthless. The beliefs of Judaism are of no value."

The Christian witness to a devout Jew should rather reflect our common roots: "We have much that binds us together. I too treasure your sacred writings as God's gift. As a Christian, I believe that they point forward to a fulfillment that occurred in Jesus Christ."

If there is any temptation to pride in our witness, we need only remind ourselves that we did absolutely nothing to deserve the treasure we have been given. If it is a mystery why God chose Abraham and the Israelites to bear his light to the world under the old covenant, it remains as much a mystery why God should use the Christian church to carry out his mission in the world under the new covenant. It was, is, and always will be a matter of grace alone.

9:1—10:39
A Better Sacrifice

9:1-10

The author now makes a smooth transition from his discussion about the covenant to a consideration of the main theme that will hold our attention all the way to the end of chapter 10. Here we come upon the second major element in the old sacrificial system—the sacrifice itself. Having established that Jesus Christ is the eternal high priest, the epistle now raises this question: can Jesus Christ also be the eternal sacrifice?

Before addressing that issue, however, the writer feels the need to raise some prior questions about the adequacy of the old sacrificial system. After a brief description of the sacrificial process itself in verses 1-5, he gives us in verse 6 a key word that can aid our understanding—the word "continually." The fact that under the old system the same sacrifices had to be repeated over and over again raises doubts about their adequacy. If the sacrifices had been complete and fully adequate they would not have been repeated. The very act of repetition under the old covenant witnesses to its own deficiency.

We have every right to ask an obvious question: Do not we do the same? Are we not urged to renew our Christian life through daily repentance? As we gather for worship each Sunday morning do not we regularly begin the service with confession and absolution? Is this any change from the ancient practice of repeating the sacrifices?

Here a careful distinction must be made between the act of confession and forgiveness on the one hand, and the resource or basis for it on the other. The need for confession and forgiveness never changes. We are as broken, sinful, and alienated from God as the people of old. As they needed renewal, so do we. As they needed an intercessor with God, so do we. As they needed a sacrifice for sin, so do we.

But the resource for forgiveness is another matter. Worshipers in the tabernacle or temple typically focused less on the mercy of God and more on the sacrificial animal or bird: as its life was given, the offerer sensed forgiveness. In time another sacrifice would need to be made.

Things are now quite different, according to the author of Hebrews. Because of the nature of the one who died, there is no need to repeat the sacrifice. The sacrifice of Christ is absolutely and completely adequate.

As we reflect on these verses we must ask: Do I tend to confess the same sins over and over again? Do I act as if certain sins are too great for God to forgive, thereby implying that the death of his Son was somehow not adequate? Do I refuse the renewal that comes with the full grace of forgiveness? Am I indeed living under the new covenant?

9:11-14

We come now to the heart of this portion of the letter. Jesus Christ, the eternal high priest, enters the heavenly holy of holies, but not with the blood of sacrificial animals. Instead he brings his own blood. He gives his own life:

> Offered was he for greatest and for least,
> Himself the victim; himself the priest.

A diagram may help us to understand these verses. Here the straight horizontal line represents time, beginning with creation on the left and terminating with the end of the world on the right. At the center of this horizontal line is a perpendicular line touching time at the bottom and reaching up into eternity at the top. A short horizontal line near the top of this vertical line forms it into the shape of a cross. Two diagonal lines from the center of the cross connect it to the beginning and to the end of the time line.

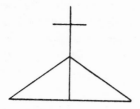

Several things emerge from the diagram:

(1) The cross touches time. Hebrews makes no attempt to lift Christ out of the world. The ultimate sacrifice occurred near the historic city of Jerusalem at a specific place called Calvary. Christ shed actual blood—his own. The suffering was intense. The death was real.

(2) The cross reaches into eternity. Because of who he is, Christ's death is no ordinary death. It is more than a mere "copy" of some ideal death in some other more perfect realm. Christ's death is in itself the perfect sacrifice.

(3) The diagonal lines reach out like an umbrella to cover the entire span of time. Christ's death on the cross is of equal efficacy for those who lived before the event and for those who live after it. Some believers looked forward to it; others look back upon it. The Christ of the Cross forgives both. His sacrifice avails for all.

The author goes on to make an intriguing distinction between "flesh" and "conscience": the old sacrifices purified the flesh, whereas the death of Christ purifies the conscience. This distinction is admittedly difficult to grasp, but its purpose is clear. It is the writer's way of saying that the impact of Christ's death is more profound. The power in this sacrifice is a reality for which the old sacrifices could only hope.

Once more the message is one that lies at the center of the New Testament: no person, no sin, no place, no time lies beyond the reach of Christ's love from the cross.

9:15–22

Death and blood! These two forbidden words occur no less than nine times in this single paragraph. In most settings we hesitate even to mention them: "I don't like to think about death!" "I can't stand the sight of blood!" Because of our normally negative attitudes toward death and blood, it is virtually impossible for us to appreciate what the author is trying to tell us.

In these verses death and blood are both seen in a positive light. Both are wholesome.

Take death for instance. There are some good things to be said about it. For one, the treasures of an inheritance pass to the heirs only when death occurs. Even though we regret and mourn the death of someone dearly loved, that person's resources, if properly disposed, do bring blessings to the people and institutions who are beneficiaries of the will.

This is the first point—that death is necessary. Unless Jesus Christ had gone to the cross the treasure of grace could not have come to us, the beneficiaries of that event. Out of his death comes life for the rest of us.

The same can be said for blood. Put yourself for the moment in the shoes of our ancient ancestors: You know little about human anatomy other than what can be learned from common observation. A comrade falls in battle, or a friend suffers serious injury, or an animal is slaughtered for food—and as the blood flows out of the body, you observe that life itself ebbs away. You naturally conclude that blood is essential to life.

Now, we have no idea when or why the idea originated that the sacrifice of an animal's life, the shedding of its blood, came to be associated with forgiveness and atonement. We know only that in the pages of the Old Testament the phrase recurs over and over again: "The life is in the blood."

If we think about it a moment, we realize that we too appreciate some things about blood. When we are desperately ill a caldron of precious gold will do us no good, but a pint of blood or a bag of plasma may save our life. In this sense we too can affirm that "the life is in the blood."

Hebrews says, "Without the shedding of blood there is no forgiveness of sins." Why sacrifice and the shedding of blood are required for forgiveness may never be clear to us. But we need not always understand the reason for something. In fact, life's most important relationships always beg for a good reason. In simple faith we can accept Jesus Christ, his sacrifice and death, as our way to the treasures of God's grace.

9:23-28

Since the beginning of Christian history, theologians studying the New Testament have come up with a variety of theories about how the death of Christ frees us from sin and overcomes the forces of evil. Most pastors have learned in seminary about these "theories of the atonement."

One of the theories suggests that Christ was offered to the devil much as an angler offers bait to a fish: with this special bait God "caught" the devil and rendered him powerless. Another theory looks at atonement the way one looks at a grocer's scale: Christ had just enough goodness to balance out the weight of evil in the world. A more recent approach sees the death of Christ in terms of power: by the power of his death he overcomes all the forces of evil. These are only three of the many theories, but they serve to illustrate the point that there are a variety of ways of thinking about the meaning of the crucifixion.

In the verses before us, the author of this epistle offers what might be considered as his theory of the atonement. The idea seems to be that for the imperfect temple under the old covenant, imperfect sacrifices would suffice. But this temple was only a "copy" of the perfect temple in which God dwells. How are we ever to enter this perfect temple? The answer, says Hebrews, is that a perfect sacrifice must be offered—and that perfect sacrifice is Jesus Christ.

What are we to make of these many theories of the atonement, including the one offered here in Hebrews? It is probably best to see each as but one facet in a many-faceted diamond. Each in its own way says something about the significance of Christ's death. But all of them taken together still cannot encompass in all its fullness the rich and profound meaning of the cross of Christ.

Like the centurion at the foot of the cross, we can do no better than to stand in awe and declare, "Truly this man was the Son of God!'' (Mark 15:39). Like Paul after he had exhausted his ways of describing God's grace in Christ, we can do no better than to confess, ''O the depth of the riches and wisdom and knowledge of God! How unsearchable are his judgments and how inscrutable his ways!'' (Rom. 11:33).

10:1–10

Some readers might think that the first eighteen verses of chapter 10 could have been omitted and we would have missed nothing, for the author seems to be repeating what he had already said clearly in chapter 9. But we can be glad these verses were not in fact omitted. In the final moments of a great organ recital there may indeed be some repetition of earlier themes, but at this part in the score they come forth with a volume and an emphasis that give flair and movement to the whole piece. And in hearing them afresh, we may even discover something a bit different from what we had noted earlier.

Here in verse 1 the writer refers to ''the law.'' Although the law has been in the background before—indeed the whole time—specific reference to it is rarely made in this epistle. What is meant here by ''the law''?

So far as we can tell, the author is thinking of law not in terms of God's great revelation of himself—a common meaning—but in terms of a narrower use that limits ''law'' to the detailed prescription which at that time governed ritual sacrifice and the civil regulations ordering community life. This law, says Hebrews, was another ''shadow'' or ''copy'' of better things to come.

The problem with the law, understood in this more restricted sense, is that it can do us no lasting good. It lacks the power to free us for useful and vibrant living.

Christians continue to discuss the role of the law in the life of the church and of the believer. Most would agree with the idea that the law in this narrower sense should have no authority over us. But what about law in the broader sense, what about the law that reveals the whole will of God, warns us about the consequences of sin, and serves as a guide for righteous living?

Christians differ at this point. Most, following the suggestion of Paul, accept the role of law in convicting us of sin and preparing us to receive Christ. But once God's grace in Christ has come to us, do we need the law anymore?

Christian opinion is divided. Some say no. Our new life is all that we need. We are so completely free, so fully guided by the Holy Spirit, that there is no more need for law at all.

Others say yes. Having been set free by Jesus Christ, we can come back to the law and respect it as a guide and a help. Christians, after all, are not free from sin and ignorance. The law can serve a good purpose in helping us to avoid sins and unwitting acts of foolishness.

Discussion about the use of the law will go on. But both sides need to recognize the common understanding that brings them together: Jesus Christ and the gospel are the heart of the church's proclamation. This is the message of Hebrews: It is not the law in any of its expressions, but Christ alone who can give freedom and joy.

10:11–18

Two little action verbs in this section say it all. Note them well:

Verse 11: "every priest *stands*";
Verse 12: "he [Christ] *sat down*."

When we stand we are normally at work and in action. With this common symbol the writer describes the priesthood under the old covenant. Because the sacrifices under the old system had to be repeated over and over again, the symbol of standing is appropriate: the demands of the law allowed for no rest.

In sharp contrast, when we sit the assumption is that our task has been completed, the work done. Because the cross is a "once and for all" act that has eternal consequences, Christ is fittingly pictured as seated, his work done. A line in the Apostles' Creed confesses that Jesus Christ is "seated at the right hand of the Father"—it may well have been drawn from this reference in Hebrews.

The other phrase from this section that catches our attention

is the quotation in verse 17, which repeats the quotation at
8:12. The words come from the prophet Jeremiah (31:34): "I
will remember their sin no more." Like Jeremiah the author of
Hebrews believes that God's grace in the new covenant is so
great and so powerful that it even allows God to forget sin that
he has forgiven. Here again, as we have noted before, our writer
friend bursts through a rather logical and reasoned line of
thought with a word that is absolute joy and light and love.

What greater good news could we hear than the message that
when God forgives he also forgets! And if he forgives so completely, why do we sometimes go on worrying about and confessing the same old sins? Why do we insist on remembering
what God has forgotten? Why do we keep bringing up what he
no longer wants to talk about? Why do we try to diminish the
power of the cross—as if that were even possible—by implying
that God's mercy is not sufficient for forgiving our sins?

10:19–25

We now come to the last of the four "sermonettes," impas-
sioned pleas that the readers return to their earlier vibrant confession. Phrases like "let us draw near" (verse 22), "let us hold
fast" (verse 23), and "let us consider" (verse 24) all convey a
sense of urgency.

The most important word, however, comes at the very end of
this section when the writer chides his readers for "neglecting to
meet together, as is the habit of some." Here is further evidence
in favor of a late-first-century date for the writing of this letter.
The believers clearly are not in the first flush of enthusiasm.
They are not new Christians, eager to worship and study.

Rather, they have fallen into neglectful habits, taking for
granted that they can always attend worship on a later occasion.
Perhaps they are second-generation or even third-generation
Christians, people who carry with them little more than a mem-
ory of what was once their parents' and their grandparents'
vibrant new faith and witness.

In our own day, when church membership falls behind pop-
ulation growth and worship attendance declines, we find these

words from Hebrews timely. The church's hardest work is not among the unchurched *outside* our walls but among the unchurched *within* our walls. Ask the evangelism committee to call on a new resident just moved into the neighborhood and they will do so eagerly. Often these newcomers are waiting for visitors from the congregation; they are eager to join the church. But calling on inactive or lapsed members is another story. After a few calls of this kind, meeting with little or no positive response, committee members sometimes conclude that this kind of calling is not their special gift and they begin looking for other tasks in the congregation. Even pastors and salaried lay workers find such calling discouraging and quickly put it at the bottom of their list of priorities. During an interim between pastorates congregational leaders are often tempted simply to drop such lapsed or lapsing members from the roll, assuming that it is of no use for anyone, even the new pastor, to work with these inactive Christians.

We need a good dose of the spirit our author is trying to convey. He obviously knows something about the discouragement of trying to revive a waning faith. But the author also recognizes what we too easily forget: these people are usually not hostile to the church. Their specific reasons for neglecting regular worship probably have nothing to do with the basics of the faith. They may be upset or angry over things that can be resolved through communication. More often than not, they simply need a word of encouragement.

Our approach to them, of course, is crucial. People often feel "used" by the church. They see the pride of the pastor and congregation over a full church, our joy over added income for paying the church's bills, our satisfaction in growing membership rolls. People can sense our selfish or superficial motivations. Our approach needs to be as straightforward as that of the author. Church members both active and inactive need to "encourage one another." With people who have been away for a time we can appeal to their need to worship and to find fellowship in the church. Absence from the gathered congregation is, as the text says, a habit that has simply developed—a *bad* habit, to be sure, but a habit nevertheless. Rather than give up on such people, we should urge them to reestablish *good* habits of worship.

10:26–31

The writer now addresses some harsh and disturbing words to people who are not simply "neglecting the faith," but who have fallen away from it. He has in mind those who "sin deliberately." Strong terms—"violated," "spurned," "profaned"—are used to characterize the intentional way in which some have turned against the faith. Continuing the use of strong language, the author says these people have "outraged the spirit of grace." One can almost feel the heat of the pen!

To such intentional apostates the reaction of God will be equally intense. Phrases like "a fearful prospect of judgment," "a fury of fire," and "without mercy" spill forth to describe how God will deal with such people. Using an analogy from the sacrifical system of the Old Testament, the writer alludes to sins for which "there no longer remains a sacrifice"—an echo of the stern warning issued back in 6:4–8, where it was declared impossible to restore someone who had committed apostasy.

Does God really act so negatively and intensely? Is the author driving his point home too hard? As we shall see in the section ahead, the writer still holds out hope for these faltering and rebellious believers. Why then such stern and judgmental language here? Why not a softer and "more loving" appeal?

It may be that our author friend knows something about "tough love." Families with chemically dependent persons surely know about it. A teen-age son is hooked on drugs. In spite of warnings from parents, siblings, friends, and counselors, he gets more and more involved in the world of chemical addiction. His parents try to be understanding and loving. No matter how bad the situation becomes, they continue to provide food, clothing, and shelter. When it becomes impossible for them to cope any longer, they enroll their son—and themselves!—in a treatment program. They begin to learn about "tough love"—the kind of love that sets standards and absolutes, talks about limits, and lays down consequences.

Finally, the eventful day comes when they must say to their

own son, "Our home is no longer your home." Then for two or three anxious days they wonder where he is. They feel guilty. They fear suicide. They are sure they have done the wrong thing. But finally the phone rings: "Hello, Mom. I'm okay. I know now that you really mean it. This time I'm going into a program by my own choice. I really want to get out of the drug scene. I want to start life over again."

A professor of mine used to put it this way: "God prefers to rule in mercy. If he cannot rule in mercy, he will rule in judgment. But rule he will!" God is not about to bend the principles of the universe to accommodate our every whim and fancy. Indeed, it *is* "a fearful thing to fall into the hands of the living God." But back of God's threats is a "tough love" that wants nothing more than that prodigal sons and daughters should come home.

10:32-39

Feeling the constraints of time, we often read books of the Bible paragraph by paragraph. That is unfortunate because by lifting a given paragraph—or chapter—out of its context we may miss the larger picture. The previous section is a case in point. Taken out of context, verses 26–31 might be taken to mean that there is little hope for Christian believers who have turned away from their earliest enthusiasm.

The succeeding verses now bring the matter into fuller perspective. True, people who repudiate the faith do bring disappointment; they do stand in danger of judgment. But hope remains alive. Like our Lord, who would not "break a bruised reed or quench a smoldering wick" (Isa. 42:3), our author looks for something that might reawaken the smoldering faith. He finds it in their past, the "former days."

Unlike those who had simply "neglected" the faith—as we saw in 2:3—these believers had apparently caved in under the pressure of harassment and persecution. Words and phrases here tumble over one another to describe those difficult times: "hard struggle with suffering," "publicly exposed to abuse and affliction," "plundering of your property."

We hear stories these days about the vitality of believers and churches in totalitarian and authoritarian societies. Christian brothers and sisters have endured the worst possible conditions without losing their faith. We point to them and recall the time-honored saying, "The blood of the martyrs is the seed of the church."

Not for a moment would any of us question the fact that hardship often brings out the best in a Christian. We must be careful, however, not to overemphasize the point. While it is true that some persecuted Christians endure, there are many others who give in to the unrelenting pressures and abandon their church and faith.

How then does one endure in hard times? The writer's advice is not: Keep the faith! Believe more! Trust more! On the contrary, he urges his readers to *act more.* Or, rather, act as you once acted! Identify with persons unjustly treated. Visit people in prison. Willingly give up your material possessions.

Whether our problem is open persecution or just a deep personal struggle with doubt, the advice is still sound. Act—even when our actions seem to have little relevance to our faith. Do the kind deed. Give "a cup of cold water." Call on someone. Audibly count your blessings—"name them one by one." Befriend someone. Give generously and sacrificially. Visit those who mourn.

Any one of us can easily think of at least a dozen people of our acquaintance who could be made happy—and probably surprised—by receiving a token of caring and kindness from us. Such people would thank us, not knowing that the blessing of such action for us has been greater than the blessing to them. If the Book of James is right and faith without works is dead, then maybe works—actions of love—can be the means by which faith is revived and renewed.

This section of Hebrews ends on a confident note. Having raised serious doubts about the steadfastness of his readers in chapters 2, 6, and now 10, the writer here exudes assurance about these same friends: "We are not of those who shrink back . . . but of those who have faith and keep their souls."

11:1—13:25
Therefore . . . Hope

11:1-2

It is important at this point in our journey through Hebrews to take note of the contrast between what we have read thus far and what remains. In essence, by the end of chapter 10 the author has completed his main line of thought. Nothing that follows relates intimately or directly to what was said earlier. In fact, beginning with chapter 11 the style of writing—and this is apparent even in the English text—is so distinct from the earlier part of the letter that most scholars think these remaining chapters were written by a different author—or authors.

Some Christians today may find it disturbing to think about the possibility of multiple authorship. It seems almost to suggest some kind of dishonesty in the origins of Scripture. If there were more than one author, why didn't they attach their signatures to what they added?

We must be careful at this point not to judge the ancient world by our contemporary standards. Apparently it was not at all uncommon in those days to add to what had been written by someone else, especially if the addition was thought to enhance the text. No rules of journalism existed to prevent it. That chapters 11—13 enrich this epistle goes without saying. In fact, we can give thanks that the Spirit of God saw fit to inspire these additions to the letter.

Let us, then, look carefully and gratefully at the single most familiar passage in Hebrews—11:1. Here in a single verse the author includes the two most fundamental aspects of all human thought and philosophy: time and space. Faith encompasses and transcends both—the "things hoped for" (time) and the "things not seen" (space).

Time has been a puzzle to humankind since the dawn of creation. The ancients were so intrigued by time that they even deified it—we have a reminder of that in "Father Time." Modern people do less philosophizing about time. In a mechanistic age that measures time in units of less than a millisecond and probes space guided by the clock of the universe, we give sparse attention to the mysteries of time. Only on rare occasions—when someone dies unexpectedly, or we reflect on the swift passing of our own days, or we vainly try to hang onto an especially beautiful moment—only then do the inexplicable secrets of time catch our attention. We cannot conceive of an existence apart from time, apart from the inexorable march from one moment to the next. We feel trapped by time.

Is there another possibility, a way of breaking the grip time has on us? Yes, says our writer. It is through faith—through trust in God, the I AM—that we are given an "assurance of things hoped for." We have an inkling of it now through Jesus Christ, the I AM who was, and is, and is to come. Our relationship with him is both time-affirming (because of his incarnation) and time-transcending (because of his resurrection). By faith we begin to experience time not only by its measurement from beginning to end, but also by its impact on a given moment. To put it another way, time is to be judged not only by its quantity, but also by its quality. A short life lived in relationship with Christ is far better than a long life lived in alienation from him.

If time is a mystery, space is fully as mysterious. As a growing lad I would sometimes lie on the grass and look up into the starry night sky: Who am I? Why am I? Where did I come from? Where am I going? Where does space begin? Where does it end? I thought and thought until I could think no more. A sense of fright would drive me into the warmth of the house and the closeness of my family.

In these past two decades humankind has made remarkable progress in answering some of our questions about space. We even talk these days about "conquering space." How ridiculous! In truth, we have advanced only a fraction of an inch toward the furthest reaches of the universe. And to our great dismay, it appears that we may already be turning back from that small venture, concentrating our resources more on the mass destruction of other members of God's family than on the peaceful exploration of the next fraction of an inch.

Yet, even if we marshaled every ounce of energy in every technology in every nation on earth for one massive thrust, we would still be overwhelmed by the invincibleness of space. We would still hear God asking us, as he asked Job, "Where were you when I laid the foundation of the earth?" (Job 38:4). And like Job, we would have to reply: "I lay my hand on my mouth" (Job 40:4).

Hebrews broaches ancient mysteries that still defy unraveling. It is by faith—by faith alone—that we have "assurance of things hoped for, the conviction of things not seen."

11:4-7

Beginning in verse 4 we enter the biblical "Hall of Faith." Starting with Abel, and sweeping through the whole history of God's people, the writer points to one person after the other who exemplifies the kind of faith described in the opening verses of the chapter. In the case of each, faith is pictured as having two elements. We see faith *in action* and faith *in the future*.

Unlike Paul, our author here sees faith more in terms of action than in terms of trust; he understands faith more as an inner quality than as a gift from outside ourselves. Abel, for example, shows his faith by acting: he offers a more acceptable sacrifice than that of his brother Cain. Enoch walks with God. Noah builds an ark. All three act on the basis of faith—without seeing the full realization of God's promise to them.

Is there a way to resolve this seeming conflict between Paul and the author of Hebrews 11? Probably not. In fact, it may be better not to try. In his wisdom God seems to have wanted more than one author to open for us the treasures of faith. Like the facets of a diamond, each author's contribution adds something to the whole. Each offers a unique insight given by the Spirit.

Paul's contribution is to help us understand that we are completely unworthy of God's grace. Like Paul, we confess: "I am the foremost of sinners" (1 Tim. 1:15). If there is anything good in us it is because "we are his workmanship, created in Christ Jesus for good works" (Eph. 2:10). Such qualities as love, joy, patience, gentleness, and self-control are called "the fruit of the Spirit" (Gal. 5:22–23) rather than natural human attributes. To Paul's way of thinking faith is the gift of trust. We are given to understand and believe that God's grace is entirely sufficient even if we have failed miserably. Faith is the foundation of Christian experience. And even at those times when we think we have responded well to God's call, we know that we remain unworthy servants, having "only done what was our duty" (Luke 17:10).

But does this understanding of faith rule out the perspective of Hebrews? Not at all. Like the author of James, our writer wants us to see that faith *as gift* must naturally evolve into faith *as action*. The examples cited here in chapter 11 all accent the idea that "faith by itself, if it has no works, is dead" (James 2:17).

There is something paradoxical about faith. On the one hand, faith alone *is* enough. The moment we add requirements beyond simple and elementary trust, we are in trouble. We are left not knowing how many requirements to add. We are left wondering whether we have met these requirements, whether we have in fact done enough, whether we have pleased God sufficiently. We are left in a quagmire of doubt.

But the other side of the paradox must not be lost: Faith alone is *not* enough. Faith calls for a response, for action. If Paul prefers to refer to the response as "good works" while the author of Hebrews prefers to call it "faith," that is of no great consequence. The point is that our author is anxious to see practical evidence that Christians have remained faithful to Christ.

Biblical faith involves both emphases. An exclusive accent on God's grace, appropriate as that might be, has at times been used by some believers as a cop-out; such persons, for example, might say, "Since I am saved by grace alone, there is need for nothing more." That is both true—since we can add nothing—and false—since faith calls for action: "Every branch of mine that bears no fruit, he takes away" (John 15:2).

11:8–22

The writer continues his list of heroes of the faith, mentioning here Abraham, Sarah, Isaac, Jacob, and Joseph. In each case the accent is on the future. These people of God acted on the faith-assumption that God is in control of the future. Acts of faith done now will help to ensure a good outcome in the future, often beyond the lifetime of the person who does the acts. Abraham left his native homeland "not knowing where he was to go." Isaac "invoked future blessings" on his twin sons. While still in Egyptian exile, Jacob blesses his grandsons, assured that God has a future for them. Joseph, still in that same exile, is so certain of his people's future that he gives instructions for his bones to be carried to the Promised Land.

Never in history has it been more important than it is today for believers to have hope for the future. At a retreat for young teen-agers a pastor asked what seemed like a normal question: "What do you hope to be doing twenty years from now?" The pastor was stunned as one after another of these young people found it impossible to answer that question. On probing deeper, the pastor learned that what made it impossible for these teen-agers to hope for anything beyond the present and the most immediate future was their anticipation of the likelihood of nuclear war.

We can hardly blame anyone—young or old—for being gloomy and pessimistic about the future. Slowly but surely it is dawning on us that nuclear weapons are not simply larger and more destructive forms of the weaponry we have had all along. They are qualitatively different—and that difference changes everything. Nuclear war has the potential not just for wiping out the past and present, as in all previous wars, but for wiping out the future as well.

Should we give in to the prevailing gloom? Should we join

those—even those believers—who no longer see a future for our world? Should we "eat, drink, and be merry, for tomorrow we die"?

The answer of faith must be an emphatic No! I will not give in. I will not lend my voice to those who write off the future of humankind. I will not act as if there is no tomorrow.

Hebrews says that these Old Testament heroes "all died in faith, not having received what was promised." Think for a moment of your own personal heroes of faith, people who are perhaps no longer in this world, whose lives served as an example for your own. Are they not like Abraham? Did any of them reach the point in life where all of their hopes had been realized? Did not most of them die with all kinds of dreams yet unfulfilled—dreams that could become reality only long after they had gone?

It is to these heroes both biblical and personal that we should look for encouragement. As they acted in the circumstances of their day, so we must act in the circumstances we face today. And let our actions be a witness to our fundamental confidence in God, that he has "the whole world in his hands," including its future. Such faith will not be passive. It will take the actions necessary to produce change, not only for today and tomorrow, but also for the long-range future.

Are we fools to believe in a God who holds the future in his control? Are we fools to hope? If so, let us be fools!

11:23–40

Here the major hero of the faith is Moses. By the time the writer finishes with Moses there is little time or space left to write at length about the other Old Testament heroes. Indeed, there is nothing to do but lump them all together and summarily credit all of them with the kinds of action that make faith evident.

Anyone familiar with the Old Testament will quickly recognize that the author of Hebrews is taking the same liberties here as he did in earlier chapters. That is to say, the exploits and faith actions of Moses, Rahab, Gideon, Barak, and others are exaggerated—stretched beyond what they actually were. Moses, for example, did not respond with enthusiasm when God called him to lead Israel out of Egypt. On the contrary, Moses offered one excuse after the other for evading the awesome task. He was hardly a model of unmitigated courage and faith. And does Rahab the prostitute really deserve to be honored with the likes of David and Samuel? Does a self-centered and cruel man like Samson belong in the same company with Gideon?

Before we go too far, however, in our judgment of the author's assessment of some of these ancient heroes, it is important to put matters into perspective. First of all, we should realize that the writer may have been relying as much on rabbinic traditions as on the books of the Old Testament itself. Those rabbinic materials tended to magnify the positive character traits of these persons, often giving them an importance that is hard to see in the Old Testament writings themselves. Furthermore, when we keep in mind that the Old Testament was not finally canonized or approved in the form we have it today until sometime after the Letter to the Hebrews was written, it is not surprising that the author may have given as much credence to the rabbinic traditions as to the Old Testament books themselves.

Another point, however, is of even greater importance: Remember our own present-day tendency to forget the negative characteristics of our faith-heroes and to magnify their good qualities. Whether our model in faith be a parent, grandparent, sibling, pastor, or friend, we, like the author of Hebrews, are inclined to remember best those aspects of their example that encourage us in our own ventures of faith and to forget the ways in which they may have fallen short. Are we being dishonest when we ignore the negative character traits and concentrate only on the positive attributes? Not necessarily. This practice of course can be carried too far, but how could even the greatest of saints serve as a good example if we always insisted on remembering their less than exemplary attitudes and actions?

There is encouragement here for all of us. In our struggles to be faithful disciples of Jesus Christ we all experience failure. Our best repeatedly falls short of our goals. In our roles as parent, neighbor, friend, employer, employee, citizen, is it not heartening to know that we will be remembered not for our worst, but for our best? Is it not another evidence of God's grace that the greatest of our faults may be forgiven and forgotten while the least of our acts of faith may be enlarged and remembered?

12:1-2

The word "therefore" is a clue that whatever follows is intimately related to what has just preceded. Thus, as we move into chapter 12 this signpost at the gate tells us that the stories of faith just reviewed are connected with what is now to be said. And the link between the two is obvious. The writer urges his readers to walk in the footsteps of those who are "so great a cloud of witnesses."

The author may have had a sports arena in mind. On the field are those believers who now live in the world. The race is on. They are to do their best. They are to set aside any "weights" that may slow them for the race. "Sin which clings so closely" is a figure of speech. The image is that of a runner who refuses to shed his tunic before the race; the long, flowing garment is sure to get tangled up in his legs, slowing his pace and causing the runner to lose.

Who are the "cloud of witnesses"? Undoubtedly the whole company of saints and believers, heroes of the faith. The writer surely has in mind also the people mentioned already in chapter 11, those saints of God who have completed their own race and now sit in the stands.

Some have wondered if people already dead can see what is going on here on earth. We sometimes hear stories about those who have "died" for a few minutes before being revived. Such survivors often describe their sensation of standing apart from their physical body to observe what is happening. Others claim to have had contact, usually through a medium, with a "departed loved one." We can only listen to their accounts, withholding judgment for lack of any way to verify the experiences they report.

Far more important than speculating about out-of-the-body experience is to understand the author's conception of the church. Death is not a wide chasm separating the community of faith here on earth from the community of the faithful departed who have died and who live again. The church on earth and the church in heaven is all one church. We sometimes describe it as being both militant (embracing those still struggling for faith here on earth) and triumphant (those who have claimed their crown of righteousness in heaven). But whatever description we prefer, the point is the same—the church is one, and the rift of death has no finality.

A powerful sense of this oneness of the church came to me several years ago as I was traveling in the country from which my great-grandparents had emigrated to America more than a century earlier. I visited the public archives where family records were kept. As I looked at those old record books holding the names of my own ancestors I felt a deep sense of gratitude for the faith that has come down through the generations. I thanked God for "a goodly heritage," a heritage that is a gift and not of my making. And I found myself deeply conscious that what I had received from my past was now laid on me as an obligation—to live out the faith in my own generation and to encourage my children to receive it for their generation and those yet to follow.

The goal, of course, lies beyond all of us. The goal of everything is Jesus Christ. He is "the pioneer and perfecter of our faith." That is to say, no matter how highly we may regard the saints of the past, from Abel or Abraham to Moses or Samuel and right down to our own time, these heroes of the faith uniformly fade in the brilliance of the greatest example of all, Jesus Christ. He, more than anyone else, exemplifies faith in action, and faith in the future. His dying on the cross stands forever as the single greatest act of trust in God. We normally see the cross in terms of the forgiveness it accomplished, the forgiveness of our sins. Here, however, we are reminded that the cross stands also as an example for us to follow, a model of patient endurance under suffering and shame.

12:3-11

This plea for endurance is again evidence for a late date of origin for the epistle. Some believers are apparently growing weary of the battle. Having resisted for so long, they are beginning to wonder if it is all worthwhile. Is faith worth the harassment that comes to a believer? Although they have not yet had to shed blood, they sense that that could happen at any time. Why not give up before it is too late?

The author urges them to think of their present suffering not only as the achievement intended by God's enemies but also as a form of discipline. God is allowing the persecution so that their faith can mature. In time they will see that the struggle was indeed worth it. They will be far stronger in faith and witness as a result of these experiences.

We sometimes think that suffering and martyrdom ended long ago, once the church was established in the early centuries. The truth of the matter is that there is more shedding of martyrs' blood today than at any time in history, though Christians in North America rarely get to see it. Even when we read about persecution in other parts of the world, we fail to comprehend it. It seems too far away to be real. Yet history tells us that no place is safe from persecution. Events change rapidly. Even in so-called Christian nations believers who seem safe and free one day can find themselves face to face with persecution the next.

Should one seek persecution and suffering? Of course not. But will it come without our seeking it? Probably it will. No matter how congenial the surrounding culture, Christian witness that expresses itself in a call for justice will inevitably meet with sharp opposition. Any culture resists change, especially if the change calls for altering a "way of life" so that more and more people will benefit from the fruits of that culture. Historically, change makers have always been regarded as the enemy. As such, they will be resisted and, if necessary, persecuted.

The church on mainland China offers a modern example of how the people of God can emerge from a time of persecution and suffering with faith intact. To be sure, many Chinese Christians caved in under recent pressure during the so-called Cultural Revolution, but many also clung to the faith and maintained their hope in the future through long years of trial. Christians around the world sometimes assumed that the church in China would have been all but wiped out during the last several decades. But as the doors of China have now opened once again we have discovered a church that has not only survived but is stronger than ever. Out of the years of "discipline" have come deeper understandings of poverty, suffering, patience, and faithfulness. There is a self-confidence and maturity in these Chinese believers that is scarcely known in cultures where the church has experienced no opposition. In China nearly one-third of the church's members are young people, born after the worst of the Communist oppression. Out of a spiritual vacuum they come looking for a word of hope.

To be sure, no Chinese Christians wish for a return to the years of persecution. Yet they know that during those long bleak years God sustained them in faith as his children. They know that "he disciplines us for our good, that we may share his holiness." They know that this suffering "later . . . yields the peaceful fruit of righteousness to those who have been trained by it."

12:12–24

This section offers a study in contrasts. The writer, as we have said, is worried that the believers may be tempted to drift back into their former ways. In order to discourage a move of that kind, he draws the lines sharply between those old ways and the way of Christ. The contrast is symbolized by Mt. Sinai and Mt. Zion. Sinai represents a blazing fire, darkness, gloom, tempest, and the voice of terror. Zion stands for the city of God, angels in festal gathering, the assembly of the firstborn, and, most important of all, the place where we meet Jesus, the mediator of the new covenant.

All of this serves to remind the readers of what had been said in 3:1—4:10. As Israel made its way to the Promised Land, so the followers of Christ are on their way to a greater Promised Land. As the going was hard for the Israelites, so it is hard for these believers in Christ. As the Israelites were tempted to turn back to Egypt, so Christians are now tempted to go back to their former ways. But going back is not the answer, says the author; going back is the road to certain disaster.

It may be, as some have observed, that the writer is here drawing too sharp a distinction between the new and the old covenants, between early Christianity and old Judiasm. He may be making the same mistake as those who see the New Testament as all gospel and the Old Testament as all law. A careful reading of the Old Testament shows that it is by no means a book of law without gospel. There is good news on almost every page—in the creation, the call of Abraham, the exodus from Egypt, the Day of Atonement, the return from exile. In all these events great and small, the Old Testament bears witness to a God of grace who loves his chosen people and keeps calling them back to himself.

Yet even when we allow for this deeper look into the Old Testament, we must still come back to a basic confession of Christian doctrine: Jesus Christ makes all the difference in the world. He stands alone, distinct from any other revelation.

In the past two or three decades we have made startling progress in Christian-Jewish relations. We still have a long way to go; with little or no encouragement anti-Semitism still rears its ugly head. But there has been movement in the right direction. Jews and Christians continue to dialogue. Together we have come to appreciate our common roots and treasures. The conversations have been good.

It must not be forgotten, however, that our Christian confession focuses on Jesus Christ as Messiah. It is this Promised One of God who sets the Christian faith apart from every other. Our differences with any particular religion must never be the basis for prejudice or disrespect. Yet the confession that "Jesus is Lord" *does* make a world of difference.

In this sense we can still say to the church: Hold fast to the faith. Don't wander off, especially in times of opposition and persecution. Consider the promises God has given you. More than anything else, consider what it means to believe that Jesus Christ is Lord.

As the world shrinks, Christianity will dialogue more and more with the non-Christian religions. And, considering the awesome forces of evil that confront humankind in a nuclear age, these conversations are of utmost importance. All people of good will, regardless of religious background, need to band together to seek peace and justice. But when all is said and done, believers must still insist that Christianity is different. The difference is a person . . . and that person is Jesus Christ!

12:25-29

The sharp contrast continues to be drawn, here in terms of responsibility. The writer recalls the awesome responsibility that had been laid on the Old Testament believers, symbolized by the fires and earthquake that accompanied the giving of the law to Moses on Mt. Sinai. The point is clear: If the *old* covenant required of Israel a high sense of responsibility, imagine the even-greater responsibility now laid on the followers of the *new* covenant.

Some students of the Letter to the Hebrews have concluded that the author has given a harsh edge to his message. The warmth and grace that fill other letters of the New Testament seem to be missing here. Appeal is made more often to repentance and judgment (the negative) than to forgiveness and grace (the positive).

Such criticism may be legitimate. But we need to put ourselves into the author's shoes and try to imagine how we would react in the same situation. The writer probably knows his readers as brothers and sisters in Christ whose faith and witness were once strong and vibrant. Where there was once high commitment and patient endurance in the face of terrible persecution, there is now ambivalence and uncertainty about the way of Christ. That being the case, is a strong word of warning out of place?

The Gospels are full of references to the responsibility that falls on those who choose to follow Jesus Christ: "Every one to whom much is given, of him will much be required" (Luke 12:48). In the parable of the talents, the master has sharp and biting words of condemnation for the man who buries his talents: "You wicked and slothful servant!" (Matt. 25:26). In his letter to the backsliding Galatians (1:8-9) Paul uses the strongest language he knows—twice—to condemn those who are leading the faithful astray. It is possible for one who has been cleansed of an evil spirit to be filled with "seven other spirits more evil" than the first (Matt. 12:45); it is possible for those who have been freed to fall away from Christ and be worse off than ever: "the last state has become worse for them than the first" (2 Peter 2:20).

I cite these New Testament references for a purpose. Whether or not the author of Hebrews leans toward a more judgmental attitude than some other New Testament authors may be a question of perspective. We should not overlook those places in the New Testament that speak about the awesome responsibilities of the Christian way and the awful consequences that come to those who backslide.

Some say that a message emphasizing judgment can alienate. They point out that, after all, a Christian congregation is a voluntary organization, and a heavy accent on responsibility and the consequences of sin will only drive people away.

Is it possible, however, that we have sold short those who belong to our churches? Is it possible that people backslide because they have had too little challenge rather than too much? Is it possible that much of the apathy we see in church life is due to our fear of confronting people with the demands of the Christian way? The new covenant comes with a much greater promise, but it also carries with it a much greater responsibility.

13:1-6

If some scholars detect a different author at work following chapter 10, practically all scholars agree that chapter 13 does not belong to the rest of the epistle. Here the contrast in style is altogether too radical, the divergence in authorship too clear. The loosely connected thoughts of chapter 13—pithy words of advice and counsel on a wide variety of subjects—were probably added to the preceding materials over a period of time by several different writers.

The opening three verses have to do with Christian hospitality, beginning with our sisters and brothers in Christ. One would assume that we could take for granted a spirit of acceptance and encouragement within the family of God's children. Unfortunately, that is not always the case. As a bishop, I find that much of my time and energy is spent resolving crises in the congregations that tend to arise out of misunderstanding and ill will between the members. Pastors too are not exempt from crisis, controversy, and conflict. Indeed ordained ministers more often than not see their fellow clergy in nearby congregations more as competitors than as partners.

Showing hospitality was especially important in early Christian times. Although there were inns all along the network of roads built by the Romans, these inns were often infested with fleas, vermin, and prostitutes. Believers therefore needed to open their own homes to those sisters and brothers in the faith who were traveling around the Mediterranean world. People who show such hospitality—now as then—sometimes find themselves hosting "angels"—guests who immeasurably enrich their own lives.

In our culture it is not unusual for both parents to be employed outside the home. Ease of travel makes it possible to be away from our homes a good deal of the time. And when we are at home, television tends to dominate our attention. The result in many instances is a loss of hospitality. How many children grow up in homes where it is the rule, rather than the exception, to have guests—and especially guests who are strangers just waiting to become friends?

The reference to prisoners in verse 3 could be misleading. We tend to think of incarcerated people almost exclusively as lawbreakers. In the first century, however, some prisoners may well have been fellow believers who, like Paul, were jailed on account of their witness for Jesus Christ. Because such people are out of sight, they are also easily out of mind. Not only should we remember them, says the author, but we must also act "as though in prison with them."

It has been suggested that verse 4, with its advice about marriage, is linked with verse 5, with its counsel regarding money. Whether that be the case or not, there is little doubt that selfishness and misunderstandings about money on the part of marriage partners are principle causes for family disintegration, separation, and divorce. "Immoral and adulterous" may refer to two different groups of people—the former unmarried and the latter married—but both are urged to live by the highest standards of sexual conduct.

As for money, we all know how it can devastate any relationship, especially within the family. Love of money, of course, is not exclusively the sin of the affluent. In fact, people with few earthly goods can as easily fall into the habit of worshiping the wealth they wish they had. The root of the problem, regardless of one's financial status, is lack of trust. For those who have *more* than others, the call is for generous giving, in trust that God will care for them. For those who gave *less* than others, the call is for courageous faith, the confidence that God will care also for them. For all of us, rich and poor alike, the call is for faithful use of all our energies and talents.

13:7–19

Much of this section, and especially verses 9–16, begs easy description. Some feel that during the early years of transmission part of the text may have been lost, thus contributing to the confusion. Others are convinced that the vague references to sacrifice may have been for the purpose of correcting faulty practices in current celebrations of the Lord's Supper.

The opening verses and closing verses, however, are clear. The readers are to pray for their leaders, recalling the heavy responsibility of those who hold office in the church. When I first entered upon my present office I felt uneasy and a bit embarrassed when I was mentioned by name in the prayers of the church: "Let us pray for Herbert, our bishop." I soon realized, however, that the prayer was entirely appropriate and that I should welcome the support of those who were praying for me. A day seldom passes when I do not have to make some decision that will have a profound effect on the lives of other persons, and more often that not on a family or congregation. I can assure you that bishops are ordinary human beings. The judgments we make are subject to human failings, weaknesses, misperceptions, pride, and selfishness. Prayers are needed and welcomed!

The same can be said regarding leaders at the local level. Pastors, lay leaders, church school teachers—everyone in a leadership position needs the intercession of the congregation.

The purpose of these prayers is to help the church's leaders live an exemplary life, a life that can serve as a model for others. Is it fair to expect these leaders to carry such responsibility? Is the example of the pastor or the deacon or the teacher more important than that of any other member?

The answer is both no and yes. No, it isn't fair to expect that a leader should be more "holy" than anyone else. The ground at the foot of the cross is level. Every church member bears responsibility for a commendable way of life.

Yet we cannot escape the fact that those who accept leadership roles in the church bear a heavier obligation to set the pace. Although confessing in one place that he is the foremost of sinners, Paul is able to say quite unashamedly, "What you have learned and received and heard and seen in me, do" (Phil. 4:9). How can the foremost of sinners invite people to follow in his footsteps? Is this not a contradiction? Not necessarily. In fact, it is questionable whether we should follow the lead of any persons who are not acutely aware of their unworthiness to be our leaders. A mark of good leaders is their admission that they too have feet of clay and need our constant prayers.

13:20-21

Although this is not the final word from the epistle, it does constitute a benediction. The fact that two completely new ideas are here introduced further testifies to the possibility of divergent authorship.

The first of these new references is to the resurrection. At no other place in the epistle is there a direct mention of Christ rising from the dead. His resurrection surely lies in the background of all that has been said, especially in those places where the eternal nature of Christ is described, but here the reference is specific: God "brought again from the dead our Lord Jesus."

Faith in the resurrected Christ is central to Christianity. Other religions have espoused ethical codes as lofty as any found in the New Testament. Sacrifice and atonement motifs appear in other religions as in Hebrews. Resurrection from the dead, however, marks Christianity as unique!

Like other pastors, I have always found the sermon for Easter Sunday the most difficult of all to prepare. What more can one say than, "He is risen! He is risen indeed!" Resurrection flies in the face of all that seems reasonable and logical. Everything appears destined for degeneration and eventual death. Nothing escapes the inexorable reality that all life must end. Little wonder, then, that Paul uses the term "foolishness" when he speaks about how the preaching of the cross sounds to those who do not believe (1 Cor. 1:18). And little wonder that he refers to the message of the resurrection as a mystery—hidden not only to unbelievers but to believers as well.

Here in Hebrews the reference to the resurrection serves to pull together many elements in the epistle. Here are people who are wavering in their faith, tired of harassment and persecution, falling back into old and more comfortable ways. To them resurrection stands as a strong challenge to hold firm. The writer is saying that if God could raise Jesus Christ from the dead, he can surely carry us through the most difficult of times.

A survey of religious attitudes illustrates how infrequently church members of our day think about resurrection. Based on a broad and representative sample of responses from a wide spectrum of religious backgrounds, the study reveals that believers tend to think about resurrection only on Easter Sunday or at the death of a loved one. Apart from Easter and funerals, church members have little consciousness of a living Christ, present and active in our world.

The other new reference in this section is to Jesus as "shepherd." Until now the letter cast Jesus in the role of high priest. Since the writer wanted to relate the life and death of Jesus Christ to the Old Testament sacrificial system, he had little choice but to use the terms familiar to that system. Here, however, as the letter comes to a close, the reference is not to the high priest but to the shepherd.

"Shepherd" conveys a warm and familiar feeling. The author tried rather successfully to give the high priest some measure of humanity and familiarity; in chapter 4 there is a beautiful allusion to the high priest as one who can sympathize with us. Yet our image of the high priest keeps him a bit distant. "Shepherd," on the other hand, bears a much stronger feeling of intimacy.

Whatever the source of the reference to Jesus as "shepherd," we can be grateful that the Letter to the Hebrews ends on this note. With strong words of warning and judgment interspersed throughout the epistle, the final allusion to a shepherd's love reminds us that God's last word to us is always a word of grace.

13:22-24

Like most letters, this one closes with a needed postscript or two—a bit of news and some personal greetings. Apparently the people reading the letter have had some contact with Timothy. The author is happy to inform them that Timothy has been released from prison. "Those who come from Italy send you greetings'' is more obscure. The sentence may mean that the letter is being written *in* Rome, or it may mean that it is being sent *to* Rome with greetings from persons who have emigrated from there to another part of the empire. What matters is that a group of believers in a local congregation are being reminded that the church is bigger than their group or congregation.

In the New Testament the Greek word for "church" is used interchangeably to describe both a local congregation and a universal fellowship. The one cannot be separated from the other. Although we experience the church locally, we are part of a family that stretches all the way around the world and even includes that "great cloud of witnesses" who have died in the faith.

It is always a temptation for members of a local congregation to become introverted and see little or no connection between themselves and the rest of God's world. Just as we are inclined individually to be turned in on ourselves, so a congregation as a corporate body is disposed to think that everything begins and ends in the local church. The temptation needs to be resisted.

Today God's family is many times larger than it was for those first-century believers. We can point now to thousands of "Timothys" who suffer for the sake of the gospel. We can join hands and hearts with contemporary "Italians"—brothers and sisters in Christ in every nation around the world.

The phrase "bear with my word of exhortation" could have several meanings. It could be a way of asking the readers to have patience while trying to assimilate what has been a rather lengthy and complex explanation of the death of Jesus Christ. As we have seen for ourselves, there are points in the letter where one would be easily tempted to put it aside because of the complicated and unusual ways in which ideas are expressed.

On the other hand, the phrase could simply be a way of softening the tone of the letter. As we have seen at several points, the awesome judgment of God is accented in order to bring faltering believers to their senses. Here at the end of the letter the author may be saying in effect, "I've had to speak some harsh words to you. I hope you will bear them patiently.

And more than anything else, I hope you will return to your earlier commitment to Jesus Christ.''

Whatever meaning we attach to the phrase, the writer clearly feels a need to add at the end a warm and personal word of encouragement. In so doing he sets a good example for all church leaders. There are times when harsh words are called for, times when God's people need to hear that he is a God of justice, times when inconsistent and unstable believers need to be brought to their senses. But the last word in the family of God's people must always be a word of love, a reminder that the Father is always ready to welcome home those who have slipped into the far country. It is fitting that this remarkable letter should end with a simple word: "Grace be with all of you. Amen.''

We have been looking into a book of the Bible that is like no other. As with Melchizedek, the epistle itself remains something of a mystery. Despite flashes of warmth here and there, it tends toward a cool and logical way of looking at the faith. In places the author's argumentation seems almost artificial. Certainly our contemporary approaches to Scripture would not allow for the liberties he takes with the Old Testament.

But as we have said, we must judge the letter by the standards of the first century rather than the twentieth. And when we do, we find that Hebrews is indeed one of the most important books in the New Testament. The Gospel writers and the apostle Paul make little effort to describe logically the meaning of the life and death of Christ. They simply proclaim it and urge their listeners to believe and trust.

The author of Hebrews, in sharp contrast, goes to great effort to "prove" that there is a connection between the old covenant and the new covenant. The death of Jesus Christ can be explained and understood if one looks at it in the right way. The death of Jesus is more than simply a sacrificial atonement for our sins, as Paul would emphasize. Whereas Paul tends to look at the ceremonial laws of the Old Testament as having been abolished by the death of Christ, the writer of Hebrews prefers to see those same laws in a more positive way. Though they indeed belong to the past, they continue to have positive value in helping to prepare for the coming of Christ.

Much more could be added about the unique way in which the epistle looks at the life and death of Jesus Christ. Behind all else, however, is the basic idea that this letter is a confession of faith. It is a confession that the coming of Jesus Christ, and especially his death, opens the way for something better, something that is superior and new. And as such it brings new hope.

We can never read the Scripture without reminding ourselves that we too are called to make a confession of faith. As the writers of the New Testament each tend to see Jesus Christ from their own perspective, so we see him with our own eye of faith. As their writings are shaped by their particular experience, so our way of confessing Christ will vary according to how we personally experience him.

But basic to every book of the New Testament, and basic also for us, is the unabashed confession that Jesus Christ—Son of God and Son of man, high priest and sacrifice—is Lord!